Practical
Hot & Spicy

p^3

This is a P³ Publishing Book
This edition published in 2004

P³ Publishing
Queen Street House
4 Queen Street
Bath BA1 1HE, UK

ISBN: 1-40543-278-0

Printed in China

NOTE

Cup measurements in this book are for American cups.
This book also uses imperial and metric measurements. Follow the same units
of measurement throughout; do not mix imperial and metric.
All spoon measurements are level: teaspoons are assumed to be 5 ml, and
tablespoons are assumed to be 15 ml. Unless otherwise stated,
milk is assumed to be whole milk, eggs and individual vegetables such as potatoes
are medium, and pepper is freshly ground black pepper.

The nutritional information provided for each recipe is per serving or per person.
Optional ingredients, variations, or serving suggestions have
not been included in the calculations. The times given for each recipe are an approximate
guide only because the preparation times may differ according to the techniques used by
different people and the cooking times may vary as a result of the type of oven used.

Recipes using raw or very lightly cooked eggs should be
avoided by infants, the elderly, pregnant women, convalescents,
and anyone suffering from an illness.

Contents

Introduction

Changing tastes and a more daring approach to what we eat have led in recent years to a growing interest in food from many different cultures. Among the most popular cuisines are those from China, India, Thailand, Mexico—anywhere, in fact, that serves hot and spicy dishes, bursting with new and exciting flavors that sometimes make your eyes water as well as your mouth. Soups, fish, meat, chicken, and vegetables are transformed with the addition of chiles, ginger, and garlic, and with a range of dried spices. The recipes in this book are quick and easy to make, but still impressive: you can create something really inspirational for a special occasion, and you can even top it off with a hot and spicy dessert.

Pantry items

In the countries from which these recipes are taken, most of the ingredients are bought absolutely fresh from the daily markets. In Thailand the diet is mostly based on fish— caught, landed, and sold within a very short time. Vegetables are also carefully chosen and purchased each day as needed.

However, there are some items that can be kept at hand. Rice is the most important staple food, either forming the basis of the entrée or, more often, served as a side dish, perhaps with herbs, spices, or vegetables added. Long-grain white rice and Indian basmati rice with its distinctive aroma and flavor are staples and readily available in large stores. They will keep for quite a while in an airtight container. Noodles are another staple, used frequently in Chinese and Thai cooking where they are tossed in a wok with meat or fish and vegetables, and seasoned generously. They come in many forms and among the most popular are rice noodles—almost transparent and shaped as flat ribbons or thin vermicelli—and the egg noodles favored by the Chinese—a rich yellow in color and crinkled in shape. Both types are not so much cooked as softened by soaking in boiling water for just a few minutes.

A range of oils is also useful, and some of these will already be kept in the pantry for general use. Sunflower oil and vegetable oil are the most widely used, because they are light and mild, complementing the food rather than flavoring it. Olive oil is commonly used in some cuisines, notably Mexican, and it is best to choose a really good extra-virgin olive oil. It is also worth investing in a bottle of sesame oil made from roasted sesame seeds and full of flavor. This is not used for cooking food because it burns easily. Instead, it is drizzled over the finished dish. And for the very brave, a bottle of chili oil is hot stuff indeed.

Beans are often used as the basis of spicy dishes because they readily absorb the delicious flavors of the food. The classic is the ever-popular Mexican chili-bean stew, warming and filling. When using beans you have two options: you can buy packages of dried beans, which are very cheap and keep well, but have to be soaked overnight before cooking; or you can buy cans of ready-cooked beans, which are a little more expensive but very useful if you want to rustle up a quick dish for lunch or for an evening dish midweek.

Also readily available, and ideal for anyone with limited spare time, are the jars of sauces and pastes stocked by food stores everywhere. Using bottled sauces is not quite the same as making them from scratch, but they still taste good. Green and red Thai curry pastes can be used for a fast green fish curry or a red lamb curry. Indian curry pastes range from mild to extremely hot. Many of the recipes in this book need dried spices, such as cumin, coriander, cardamom, and turmeric. Their

flavor deteriorates rapidly, so, unless you are planning to do a lot of this type of cooking, buy them in small quantities and store them in a cool, dark place. Also add some authentic seasoning sauces to your pantry—soy sauce, which is made from fermented soy beans, and Thai fish sauce, which is made from salted fermented fish.

Chiles, ginger, and garlic

All these items add a real zing to your hot and spicy cooking, but it is fair to say that when it comes to heat, chiles are the star. There are many varieties of chile, and different cultures favor different ones, so it is worth looking out for the right one for a particular dish. Many recipes call for chiles, but dried, crushed chilies may be substituted. Some chiles are quite mild, while others are fiery hot—large chiles are usually milder than small ones, and red chiles tend to be a little sweeter and milder than green ones. If you are in any doubt about eating a dish seasoned with chiles, bear in mind that most of the heat is in the seeds. If you remove the seeds before cooking, the dish will not be so fiery.

Thai dishes often include bird-eye chiles. These are small and either red or green, and they are very, very hot. In Mexico, where chiles of one variety or another are included in virtually every recipe, the small, green variety called *jalapeño* is especially popular, and dried chilies—*ancho* and *chipotle*—are also used.

Chiles are extremely irritating to the skin, so if you are particularly sensitive, wear rubber gloves when preparing them, and if you are removing the seeds, do so with the point of a sharp knife. Always wash your hands really thoroughly afterward, and make sure you keep your hands away from your eyes.

Fresh ginger is a marvelous spice, adding flavor as well as fire. Substituting the dried, powdered ginger used in baking is out of the question. The fresh or "green" root is sold in food stores everywhere, however, and your only problem may be in identifying it. It is quite small and very knobbly, similar to a Jerusalem artichoke in shape and color, and it should feel firm to the touch.

When the root is peeled, the yellow flesh is revealed and the delicious aroma wafts out. Ginger is usually grated and thrown into the wok at the start of cooking a stir-fry, infusing the oil with its marvelous flavor.

Garlic, crushed or chopped, is used throughout the world, and not just for spicy cooking, so fresh garlic is usually readily available. It is a bulb formed of edible cloves packed tightly around an inedible core. Garlic's reputation for tainting the breath is unfortunately entirely justified, but you may decide that the special flavor and subtle kick it imparts is worth it—chewing parsley or caraway seeds is said to reduce the odor.

Cooking utensils

There is no essential piece of equipment needed for hot and spicy cuisine—your usual cooking pans and a good heavy skillet will be all you need—but if you intend to do a lot of spicy cooking, a wok is a very useful item of equipment to have in the kitchen.

The wok is a Chinese cooking pan. It is shallow and convex in shape, allowing the heat to spread evenly, especially if it sits on a "collar" over the heat source. It is ideal for stir-frying because the curved sides make it easy to toss food as it cooks. For this you need a spatula with a long wooden handle to insulate your hand from the heat. Although they are pricey, it is worth investing in a cast-iron wok, because these are most effective at retaining heat—and fast cooking is the key to successful stir-frying.

The wok is at its best when well seasoned. To do this, wipe it inside and out with oil, then bring it up to a high temperature on a stove. Repeat this a few times to coat it well. The seasoned wok will then only need to be wiped after use, then cleaned with detergent and water and dried immediately to prevent rusting.

KEY

 Simplicity level 1–3 (1 easiest, 3 slightly harder)

 Preparation time

 Cooking time

Mexican Chili Soup

This soup evolved from the food stalls that line the streets of Tlalpan, a suburb of Mexico City. It contains avocado, chicken, and chipotle chilies.

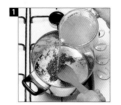

NUTRITIONAL INFORMATION

Calories	218	Sugars	. . . . .1g
Protein	. . . . .28g	Fat	. . . . .11g
Carbohydrate	. . . .2g	Saturates	. . . . . . .2g

15 mins   0 mins

SERVES 4

I N G R E D I E N T S

6⅓ cups chicken bouillon

2–3 garlic cloves, finely chopped

1–2 chipotle chilies, cut into very thin strips (see Cook's Tip)

1 avocado

lime or lemon juice, for tossing

3–5 scallions, thinly sliced

12–14 oz/350–400 g cooked chicken breast meat, torn, or cut into shreds or thin strips

2 tbsp chopped fresh cilantro

TO SERVE

1 lime, cut into wedges

handful of tortilla chips (optional)

1 Pour the bouillon in a large pan, with the garlic and the chipotle chilies, and bring to a boil.

2 Meanwhile, cut the avocado in half around the pit. Twist apart, then remove the pit with a knife. Carefully peel away the skin, dice the flesh, and toss it gently in lime or lemon juice to prevent discoloration.

3 Arrange the scallions, chicken, avocado, and cilantro in the bottom of 4 soup bowls or in a large serving bowl.

4 Ladle the hot bouillon over the ingredients in the bowls, and serve with wedges of lime, and a handful of tortilla chips, if using.

COOK'S TIP

Chipotle chilies are smoked and dried jalapeño chiles and are available canned or dried.

Hot & Sour Soup

Hot-and-sour mixtures are popular throughout the East, especially in Thailand. This soup typically has either shrimp or chicken added.

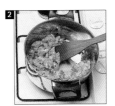

NUTRITIONAL INFORMATION

Calories	71	Sugars	. . . . . . .0.1g
Protein	. . . . .8g	Fat	. . . . .4g
Carbohydrate	. . . .1g	Saturates	. . . . .0.1g

🧊 30 mins   🕐 25 mins

SERVES 4

I N G R E D I E N T S

12 oz/350 g whole raw or cooked shrimp in their shells

1 tbsp vegetable oil

1 lemongrass stem, coarsely chopped

2 kaffir lime leaves, shredded

1 green chile, seeded and chopped

5 cups chicken or fish bouillon

1 lime

1 tbsp Thai fish sauce

1 red bird-eye chile, seeded and thinly sliced

1 scallion, thinly sliced

salt and pepper

1 tbsp finely chopped fresh cilantro, to garnish

1 Peel the shrimp and reserve the shells. Devein the shrimp, cover, and chill.

2 Heat the oil in a large pan and stir-fry the shrimp shells for 3–4 minutes, until they turn pink. Add the lemongrass, lime leaves, green chile, and bouillon. Grate the zest from the lime and add to the pan.

3 Bring to a boil, then lower the heat, cover, and simmer the bouillon gently for about 20 minutes.

4 Strain the liquid, then pour it back into the pan. Squeeze the juice from the lime and add to the pan with the fish sauce, and salt and pepper to taste.

5 Bring the soup to a boil. Lower the heat, add the shrimp, and simmer for just 2–3 minutes.

6 Add the red chile and sliced scallion. Sprinkle with cilantro and serve.

COOK'S TIP

To devein the shrimp, first remove the shells. Cut a slit along the back of each shrimp and remove the fine black vein that runs along the length of the back. Wipe each shrimp with clean paper towels.

Authentic Guacamole

Guacamole is at its best when it is freshly made. Serve it as a sauce with anything Mexican, or as a dip for raw vegetable sticks or tortilla chips.

NUTRITIONAL INFORMATION

Calories	212	Sugars	. . . . .1g
Protein	. . . . .2g	Fat	. . . . .21g
Carbohydrate	. . . .3g	Saturates	. . . . . . .4g

 15 mins   0 mins

SERVES 4

I N G R E D I E N T S

1 ripe tomato

2 limes

2–3 ripe, small to medium avocados, or 1–2 large ones

¼–½ onion, finely chopped

pinch of ground cumin

pinch of mild chili powder

½–1 green chile, such as jalapeño or serrano, seeded and finely chopped

1 tbsp finely chopped fresh cilantro, plus extra to garnish

salt (optional)

tortilla chips, to serve (optional)

 1 First skin the tomato: place it in a bowl, cover with boiling water, and let stand for 30 seconds. Drain and plunge

COOK'S TIP

Avocados grow in abundance in Mexico, and guacamole is used to add richness and flavor to all manner of dishes. Try spooning it into soups, especially chicken or seafood, or spreading it into sandwiches or on thick, crusty rolls.

the tomato into cold water. The skin will then slide off easily. Cut in half, seed, and chop the tomato flesh.

2 Squeeze the juice from the limes into a small bowl. Cut the avocados in half around the pits. Twist apart, then remove the pits with a knife. Carefully peel off the skin, dice the flesh, and toss in the bowl of lime juice to prevent them from discoloring. Mash the avocados coarsely.

3 Add the onion, tomato, cumin, chili powder, chopped chiles, and chopped cilantro to the mashed avocados. If the guacamole is to be used as a dip for tortilla chips, do not add salt. If it is to be used as a sauce, add salt to taste.

4 To serve the guacamole as a dip, transfer it to a serving dish, garnish with finely chopped cilantro, and serve with tortilla chips for dipping.

Grilled Eggplant

Eggplants grow easily throughout the Far East and they are a popular vegetable in Thailand. This dish works well as an appetizer.

NUTRITIONAL INFORMATION

Calories 106   Sugars 6g
Protein . . . . .3g   Fat 8g
Carbohydrate . . . .7g   Saturates 1g

20 mins, plus
50 mins salting   10 mins
and marinating

SERVES 4

I N G R E D I E N T S

8 baby eggplants

salt, for salting eggplants

2 tsp chili oil

1 tbsp soy sauce

1 tbsp Thai fish sauce

1 garlic clove, thinly sliced

1 red bird-eye chile, seeded and sliced

1 tbsp sunflower oil

1 tsp sesame oil

1 tbsp lime juice

1 tsp soft, light brown sugar

1 tbsp fresh mint, chopped

1 tbsp sesame seeds, toasted

fresh mint leaves, to garnish

1 Cut the eggplants lengthwise into thin slices to within 1 inch/2.5 cm of the stem end. Place the slices in a colander, sprinkle salt between them, and let drain for about 30 minutes. Rinse under cold running water, then pat completely dry with paper towels.

2 Mix the chili oil, soy sauce, and fish sauce and brush over the eggplants. Cook under a hot broiler, or barbecue over hot coals, for 6–8 minutes, turning occasionally and brushing with chili glaze, until golden and softened. Arrange the eggplants on a large serving platter.

3 Cook the sliced garlic and chile in the sunflower oil for 1–2 minutes, until they just begin to brown. Remove from the heat and add the sesame oil, lime juice, sugar, and any remaining chili oil glaze.

4 Add the chopped mint and spoon the warm dressing over the eggplants.

5 Let marinate for about 20 minutes, then sprinkle with toasted sesame seeds. Serve garnished with mint leaves.

Spicy Lentils & Spinach

This is a filling dish, which should be served with just a light entrée or as a one-dish lunch or supper. Field green peas are a type of lentil.

NUTRITIONAL INFORMATION

Calories 355	Sugars 7g	
Protein 20g	Fat 16g	
Carbohydrate . . .35g	Saturates 2g	

🥄 10 mins, plus 2 hrs soaking   🕐 35 mins

SERVES 4

I N G R E D I E N T S

1 cup field green peas

2 lb/900 g spinach

4 tbsp vegetable oil

1 onion, halved and sliced

1 tsp grated fresh gingerroot

1 tsp ground cumin

½ tsp chili powder

½ tsp ground coriander

2 garlic cloves, crushed

1¼ cups vegetable bouillon

salt and pepper

TO GARNISH

sprigs of fresh cilantro

lime wedges

1 Rinse the field peas under cold running water. Transfer to a bowl, cover with cold water, and soak for 2 hours. Drain well.

2 Meanwhile, cook the spinach in a large pan for 5 minutes, until wilted. Drain well and chop coarsely.

3 Heat the oil in a large pan and sauté the onion, spices, and garlic. Sauté for 2–3 minutes, stirring well.

4 Add the field peas and spinach and stir in the bouillon. Cover and simmer for 10–15 minutes, or until the field peas are cooked and the liquid has been absorbed. Season with salt and pepper to taste, garnish with sprigs of cilantro and wedges of lime, and serve.

VARIATION

If you do not have time to soak the field peas, canned baby lentils (drained) are a good substitute.

Mexican Potato Salad

This dish is full of enticing Mexican flavors. Potato slices are topped with tomatoes, chile, and bell peppers, and served with a guacamole dressing.

NUTRITIONAL INFORMATION

Calories	260	Sugars	.........6g
Protein	.........6g	Fat	...........9g
Carbohydrate	...41g	Saturates	......2g

10 mins, plus 30 mins cooling   15 mins

SERVES 4

INGREDIENTS

4 large waxy potatoes, sliced

1 ripe avocado

1 tsp olive oil

1 tsp lemon juice

1 garlic clove, crushed

1 onion, chopped

2 large tomatoes, sliced

1 green chile, chopped

1 yellow bell pepper, seeded and cut into strips

2 tbsp chopped fresh cilantro

salt and pepper

lemon wedges, to garnish

1 Cook the potatoes in a pan of boiling water for 15 minutes. Drain and cool.

2 Meanwhile, cut the avocado in half and remove the pit. Using a spoon, scoop the avocado flesh from the 2 halves and place in a mixing bowl.

3 Mash the avocado flesh with a fork. Stir in the olive oil, lemon juice, garlic, and onion. Cover the bowl and set aside.

4 Mix the tomatoes, chile, yellow bell pepper, and potato slices, then divide them between serving plates.

5 Spoon the avocado mixture on top of the salad base and sprinkle over the cilantro. Season to taste and serve garnished with lemon wedges.

COOK'S TIP

Choose a ripe avocado that yields to gentle pressure from your thumb. Mixing the avocado flesh with lemon juice prevents it from turning brown once exposed to the air.

Stir-Fried Ginger Mushrooms

This quick vegetarian stir-fry is somewhat like a rich curry. It is full of warm spices and garlic, and the flavors are balanced with creamy coconut milk.

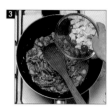

NUTRITIONAL INFORMATION

Calories	174	Sugars	.........7g
Protein	.........8g	Fat	...........9g
Carbohydrate	...15g	Saturates	.......1g

 10 mins   🕐 10 mins

SERVES 4

I N G R E D I E N T S

2 tbsp vegetable oil

3 garlic cloves, crushed

1 tbsp Thai red curry paste

½ tsp turmeric

15 oz/425 g canned Chinese straw mushrooms, drained and halved

¾-inch/2-cm piece fresh gingerroot, finely shredded

scant ½ cup coconut milk

1 cup dried Chinese black mushrooms, soaked, drained, and sliced

1 tbsp lemon juice

1 tbsp light soy sauce

2 tsp sugar

½ tsp salt

8 cherry tomatoes, halved

7 oz/200 g firm bean curd, diced

fresh cilantro leaves, to garnish

boiled fragrant rice, to serve

COOK'S TIP

You can vary the mushrooms depending on your own taste. Try a mixture of oyster and shiitake for a change—or use cultivated white mushrooms.

1 Heat the oil in a pan and cook the garlic for about 1 minute, stirring constantly. Stir in the curry paste and turmeric, and cook for another 30 seconds.

2 Add the straw mushrooms and ginger, and stir-fry for 2 minutes. Stir in the coconut milk and bring to a boil. Add the Chinese black mushrooms, lemon juice, soy sauce, sugar, and salt, stir well, and heat thoroughly.

3 Add the tomatoes and bean curd and toss gently to heat through.

4 Scatter the cilantro over the mixture and serve hot with freshly boiled rice.

Spiced Cashew Curry

This unusual vegetarian dish may be served on its own with rice, but can also be presented as a side dish with other vegetables or with meat.

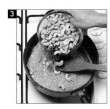

NUTRITIONAL INFORMATION

Calories	455	Sugars	........6g
Protein	........13g	Fat	..........39g
Carbohydrate	...16g	Saturates	......11g

🌶 15 mins, plus 8 hrs soaking   🕐 20 mins

SERVES 4

I N G R E D I E N T S

1⅔ cups unsalted cashews

1 tsp coriander seeds

1 tsp cumin seeds

2 cardamom pods, crushed

1 tbsp sunflower oil

1 onion, finely sliced

1 garlic clove, crushed

1 small green chile, seeded and chopped

1 cinnamon stick

½ tsp ground turmeric

4 tbsp coconut cream

1¼ cups hot vegetable bouillon

3 kaffir lime leaves, finely shredded

salt and pepper

boiled jasmine rice, to serve

1 Soak the cashews in cold water overnight. Drain thoroughly. Crush the coriander seeds, cumin seeds, and cardamom pods in a spice grinder or with a pestle and mortar.

2 Heat the oil in a large skillet and stir-fry the onion and garlic for 2–3 minutes, until they are soft but not brown. Add the chopped chile, crushed spices, cinnamon stick, and ground turmeric, and stir-fry for another minute.

3 Add the coconut cream and the hot bouillon to the pan. Bring to a boil, then add the cashews and lime leaves, and salt and pepper to taste.

4 Cover the pan, lower the heat, and simmer for about 20 minutes. Remove and discard the cinnamon stick. Serve hot with freshly cooked jasmine rice.

COOK'S TIP

You can always use ready-ground spices for speed, but all spices will give a better flavor if you crush them just before use in a spice grinder or with a pestle and mortar.

Potato-Filled Nans

This is a filling sandwich made with Indian bread. Spicy potatoes fill the nans, which are served with a cool cucumber raita and lime pickle.

NUTRITIONAL INFORMATION

Calories	244	Sugars	.........7g
Protein	.........8g	Fat	...........8g
Carbohydrate	...37g	Saturates	......1g

🥔 10 mins   🕐 25 mins

SERVES 4

I N G R E D I E N T S

8 oz/225 g waxy potatoes, scrubbed and diced

1 tbsp vegetable oil

1 onion, chopped

2 garlic cloves, crushed

1 tsp ground cumin

1 tsp ground coriander

½ tsp chili powder

1 tbsp tomato paste

3 tbsp vegetable bouillon

2¾ oz/75 g baby spinach, shredded

4 small or 2 large nans

lime pickle, to serve

R A I T A

⅔ cup lowfat plain yogurt

4 tbsp diced cucumber

1 tbsp chopped mint

1 Cook the diced potatoes in a pan of boiling water for 10 minutes. Drain thoroughly.

2 Heat the vegetable oil in a separate pan and cook the onion and garlic for 3 minutes, stirring. Add the spices and cook for another 2 minutes.

3 Add the partially cooked potatoes, with the tomato paste, vegetable bouillon, and spinach, and stir to mix. Cook for 5 minutes, until the potatoes are tender.

4 Warm the nans in a preheated oven, 300°F/150°C, for about 2 minutes.

5 To make the raita, mix the yogurt, cucumber, and mint together in a small bowl.

6 Remove the nans from the oven. Using a sharp knife, cut a pocket in the side of each. Spoon some of the spicy potato mixture into each pocket.

7 Serve the filled nans at once, accompanied by the raita and lime pickle.

COOK'S TIP

To give the raita a much stronger flavor, make it in advance and let chill in the refrigerator, until you are ready to serve the meal.

Migas

A delicious brunch or late-night supper dish, this is made by scrambling eggs with chiles, tomatoes, and crisp tortilla chips.

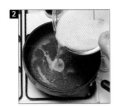

NUTRITIONAL INFORMATION

Calories 441	Sugars 5g	
Protein 22g	Fat 20g	
Carbohydrate . . .46g	Saturates 8g	

10 mins   10 mins

SERVES 4

INGREDIENTS

2 tbsp butter

6 garlic cloves, finely chopped

1 fresh green chile, such as jalapeño or serrano, seeded and diced

1½ tsp ground cumin

6 ripe tomatoes, coarsely chopped

8 eggs, lightly beaten

8–10 corn tortillas, cut into strips and fried until crisp, or an equal amount of not-too-salty tortilla chips

4 tbsp chopped fresh cilantro

3–4 scallions, thinly sliced

mild chili powder, to garnish

1 Melt half the butter in a pan. Add the garlic and chile and cook until softened but not browned. Add the cumin and cook for 30 seconds, stirring, then add the tomatoes and cook over medium heat for an additional 3–4 minutes, or until the tomato juices have evaporated. Remove from the pan and set aside.

2 Melt the remaining butter in a skillet over low heat and pour in the beaten eggs. Cook gently, stirring, until the egg begins to set.

3 Add the chile and tomato mixture, stirring gently to mix into the eggs.

4 Carefully add the tortilla strips or chips and continue cooking, stirring once or twice, until the eggs have reached the consistency you desire. The tortillas should be pliable and chewy.

5 Transfer the mixture to a serving plate and surround it with the chopped cilantro and sliced scallions. Garnish with a sprinkling of mild chili powder and serve immediately.

COOK'S TIP

Serve the migas with sour cream or crème fraîche on top, to melt seductively into the spicy eggs.

Mixed Vegetable Balti

Any combination of vegetables or beans can be used in this recipe.
It would make a good dish to serve to vegetarians.

NUTRITIONAL INFORMATION

Calories 207   Sugars 6g
Protein . . . . .8g   Fat 9g
Carbohydrate . . .24g   Saturates 1g

 10 mins   1 hr 10 mins

SERVES 4

I N G R E D I E N T S

1 cup field yellow peas, washed

3 tbsp oil

1 tsp onion seeds

2 onions, sliced

4½ oz/125 g zucchini, sliced

4½ oz/125 g potatoes, cut into
   ½-inch/1-cm cubes

4½ oz/125 g carrots, sliced

1 small eggplant, sliced

8 oz/225 g tomatoes, chopped

1¼ cups water

3 garlic cloves, chopped

1 tsp ground cumin

1 tsp ground coriander

1 tsp salt

2 fresh green chiles, sliced

½ tsp garam masala

2 tbsp chopped fresh cilantro

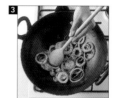

1 Put the field peas into a pan and cover with salted water. Bring to a boil and simmer for 30 minutes. Drain the peas and keep warm.

2 Heat the oil in a balti pan or a wok, and when it reaches high heat, add the onion seeds. Keeping the heat high, cook them until they start popping.

3 Add the sliced onions and stir-fry until softened and golden brown.

4 Add the prepared zucchini, potatoes, carrots, and eggplant to the pan, and stir-fry for 2 minutes.

5 Stir in the chopped tomatoes, water, chopped garlic, ground cumin, ground coriander, salt, sliced chiles, garam masala, and the reserved field peas.

6 Bring to a boil, then simmer for 15 minutes, stirring from time to time, until all the vegetables are tender.

7 Stir the cilantro into the vegetables and serve.

Thai-Spiced Salmon

Marinated in delicate Thai spices and quickly pan-fried to perfection, these salmon fillets are a perfect dish for a special dinner.

NUTRITIONAL INFORMATION

Calories . . . . . . .329 Sugars 0.1g
Protein . . . . .30g Fat 23g
Carbohydrate . . .0.1g Saturates 4g

15 mins, plus
30 mins chilling   5 mins

SERVES 4

I N G R E D I E N T S

1-inch/2.5-cm piece grated fresh gingerroot

1 tsp coriander seeds, crushed

¼ tsp chili powder

1 tbsp lime juice

1 tsp sesame oil

4 medium salmon fillets, skin left on

2 tbsp vegetable oil

T O   S E R V E

freshly boiled rice

stir-fried vegetables

1 Mix the grated gingerroot with the crushed coriander seeds and the chili powder in a small bowl. Add the lime juice and sesame oil.

COOK'S TIP

It is important to use a skillet or a ridged grill pan for this recipe, so the fish cooks evenly throughout without sticking. If the fish is very thick, turn it carefully to cook on the other side for 2–3 minutes.

2 Place the salmon fillets, skin side down and side by side, on a wide, nonmetallic plate or dish. Spoon over the spice mixture, spreading to coat evenly.

3 Cover the dish with plastic wrap and chill the salmon in the refrigerator for 30 minutes to let the flavors penetrate.

4 Pour the oil into a wide, heavy-bottomed skillet or ridged grill pan and heat it to a high temperature. Place the salmon on the hot pan, skin side down.

5 Cook the salmon for 4–5 minutes, without turning, until the fillets are crusty underneath and the flesh flakes easily. Transfer immediately to warmed plates and serve at once with the boiled rice and stir-fried vegetables.

Shrimp Skewers with Chile

Whole jumbo shrimp cook very quickly on a barbecue grill or under a broiler, so they are ideal for summertime cooking, indoors or outside.

NUTRITIONAL INFORMATION

Calories	106	Sugars	8g
Protein	11g	Fat	3g
Carbohydrate	8g	Saturates	1g

🍲 5 mins, plus 2 hrs marinating ⏱ 6 mins

SERVES 4

I N G R E D I E N T S

1 garlic clove, chopped

1 red bird-eye chile, seeded and chopped

1 tbsp tamarind paste

1 tbsp sesame oil

1 tbsp dark soy sauce

2 tbsp lime juice

1 tbsp soft, light brown sugar

16 raw jumbo shrimp

1 lime, cut into wedges

TO SERVE

fresh crusty bread

fresh salad greens

1 Put the chopped garlic and chile in a small pan with the tamarind paste, sesame oil, soy sauce, lime juice, and sugar. Stir over low heat until the sugar has completely dissolved, then remove from the heat, and let cool.

2 Wash and pat dry the shrimp and place in a single layer in a wide, nonmetallic dish. Spoon the marinade over the shrimp and turn them over to coat evenly. Cover the dish with plastic wrap and let marinate in the refrigerator for at least 2 hours, or preferably overnight.

3 When you are almost ready to cook the shrimp, soak 4 bamboo or wooden skewers in water for about 20 minutes. Drain and dry the skewers, then thread 4 shrimp onto each skewer.

4 Broil the skewered shrimp under a preheated hot broiler for 5–6 minutes, turning them once, until they turn pink and begin to turn brown. Alternatively, barbecue over hot coals.

5 Thread a wedge of lime onto the end of each skewer and serve with fresh crusty bread and salad greens.

Chicken Jalfrezi

This is a quick and tasty way of using leftover roast chicken. The sauce can also be used to accompany any cooked poultry, lamb, or beef.

NUTRITIONAL INFORMATION

Calories 270	Sugars 3g	
Protein 36g	Fat 11g	
Carbohydrate 7g	Saturates 2g	

25 mins   15 mins

SERVES 4

I N G R E D I E N T S

1 tsp mustard oil

3 tbsp vegetable oil

1 large onion, finely chopped

3 garlic cloves, crushed

1 tbsp tomato paste

2 tomatoes, skinned and chopped

1 tsp ground turmeric

½ tsp cumin seeds, ground

½ tsp coriander seeds, ground

½ tsp chili powder

½ tsp garam masala

1 tsp red wine vinegar

1 small red bell pepper, seeded and chopped

1 cup frozen fava beans

1 lb 2 oz/500 g cooked chicken, cut into bite-size pieces

salt

sprigs of fresh cilantro, to garnish

freshly cooked basmati rice, to serve

1 Heat the mustard oil in a large skillet set over high heat for about 1 minute, until it begins to smoke.

2 Add the vegetable oil, lower the heat, and then add the onion and the garlic. Cook them gently until they are softened and golden.

3 Add the tomato paste, chopped tomatoes, turmeric, ground cumin and coriander seeds, chili powder, garam masala, and red wine vinegar to the skillet. Stir the mixture over the heat, until fragrant.

4 Add the red bell pepper and fava beans and stir for 2 minutes, until the pepper is softened. Stir in the chicken and add salt to taste.

5 Simmer gently for 6–8 minutes, until the chicken is heated through and the beans are tender.

6 Serve immediately, garnished with sprigs of fresh cilantro and accompanied by freshly cooked basmati rice.

Chicken & Mango Stir-Fry

This dish has a colorful, exotic mix of flavors that works surprisingly well. It is easy and quick to cook—ideal for a midweek family meal.

NUTRITIONAL INFORMATION

Calories . . . . . . .200 Sugars 5g
Protein . . . . .23g Fat 6g
Carbohydrate . . . .7g Saturates 1g

15 mins   15 mins

SERVES 4

I N G R E D I E N T S

6 skinless, boneless chicken thighs

2 tsp grated fresh gingerroot

1 garlic clove, crushed

1 small red chile, seeded

1 large red bell pepper

4 scallions

7 oz/200 g snow peas

3½ oz/100 g baby corn cobs

1 large, firm, ripe mango

2 tbsp sunflower oil

1 tbsp light soy sauce

3 tbsp rice wine or sherry

1 tsp sesame oil

salt and pepper

snipped chives, to garnish

1 Cut the chicken into long, thin strips and place in a bowl. Mix together the ginger, garlic, and chile, then stir into the chicken strips to coat them evenly.

2 Slice the red bell pepper thinly, then cut it diagonally. Trim the scallions and slice them diagonally. Cut the snow peas and corn cobs in half diagonally. Peel the mango, remove the pit, and slice thinly.

3 Heat the oil in a large skillet or wok over high heat. Add the chicken and stir-fry for 4–5 minutes, until just turning golden brown. Add the bell pepper and stir-fry over medium heat for 4–5 minutes to soften.

4 Add the scallions, snow peas, and corn cobs, and stir-fry for an additional minute.

5 Mix together the soy sauce, rice wine or sherry, and sesame oil, and stir into the wok. Add the mango and stir gently for 1 minute to heat thoroughly.

6 Adjust the seasoning with salt and pepper to taste and serve immediately, garnished with chives.

Chicken with Vinegar

Roasted garlic and mixed spices give an evocative flavor to this tangy chicken dish, a specialty of Valladolid in the Yucatan peninsula.

NUTRITIONAL INFORMATION

Calories . . . . .313 Sugars 6g
Protein . . . . .15g Fat 22g
Carbohydrate . . .14g Saturates 3g

20 mins,
plus 1 hr
marinating   25 mins

SERVES 4

I N G R E D I E N T S

8 small, boned chicken thighs

about 2½–3 cups chicken bouillon

15–20 garlic cloves, unpeeled

1 tsp coarsely ground black pepper

½ tsp ground cloves

2 tsp crumbled dried oregano or ½ tsp
crushed or powdered bay leaves

½ tsp salt

1 tbsp lime juice

1 tsp cumin seeds, lightly toasted

1 tbsp flour, plus extra for dredging
the chicken

3–4 onions, thinly sliced

2 chiles, preferably mildish yellow ones,
such as Mexican güero or similar Turkish
or Greek chiles, seeded and sliced

1 cup vegetable oil

scant ½ cup cider vinegar or sherry vinegar

1 Place the chicken in a pan with enough bouillon to cover. Bring to a boil, then reduce the heat and simmer for 5 minutes. Remove from the heat and let the chicken cool and continue to cook in the bouillon.

2 Meanwhile, roast the garlic cloves in a dry skillet until they are lightly browned on all sides and tender inside. Let cool, then squeeze the flesh from the skins.

3 Grind together the garlic, black pepper, cloves, oregano, salt, lime juice, and ¾ teaspoon of the cumin seeds. Add 1 tablespoon of flour.

4 When the chicken is cool, remove from the bouillon and pat dry. Reserve the bouillon. Rub the chicken with about two-thirds of the garlic-spice paste, and marinate for 1–12 hours in the refrigerator.

5 Cook the onions and chiles in a little of the oil, until golden brown. Pour in the vinegar and remaining cumin seeds, cook for a few minutes, then add the reserved bouillon and remaining spice paste. Continue to cook, stirring, for 10 minutes.

6 Dredge the chicken in flour. Cook in the remaining oil until lightly browned. Serve with the onion mixture.

Chicken Tikka

The secret of this very popular dish is that small pieces of chicken are marinated for a minimum of 3 hours in yogurt, garlic, and fragrant spices.

NUTRITIONAL INFORMATION

Calories	327	Sugars	.........2g
Protein	........61g	Fat	..........8g
Carbohydrate	....3g	Saturates	.......1g

15 mins, plus 3 hrs marinating   10 mins

SERVES 6

I N G R E D I E N T S

1 tsp finely chopped fresh gingerroot

1 tsp crushed fresh garlic

½ tsp ground coriander

½ tsp ground cumin

1 tsp chili powder

3 tbsp yogurt

1 tsp salt

2 tbsp lemon juice

a few drops of red food coloring (optional)

1 tbsp tomato paste

3 lb 5 oz/1.5 kg chicken breast

1 onion, sliced

3 tbsp oil

TO SERVE

fresh salad greens

1 lemon, cut into wedges

warm nan bread

3 Using a sharp knife, cut the chicken into bite-size pieces. Add the chicken pieces to the spice mixture and toss to coat well. Let marinate for as long as possible—for a minimum of 3 hours or, if possible, overnight.

4 Arrange the onion in the bottom of a heatproof dish. Carefully drizzle half of the oil over the onions.

5 Arrange the marinated chicken pieces on top of the onions and cook under a preheated broiler, turning once and basting with the remaining oil, for approximately 10 minutes, until the chicken is cooked through and tender.

6 Serve on a bed of fresh salad greens with warm nans, and lemon wedges for squeezing.

1 Mix the ginger, garlic, coriander, cumin, and chili powder thoroughly in a large mixing bowl.

2 Add the yogurt, salt, lemon juice, red food coloring (if using), and tomato paste to the mixing bowl.

 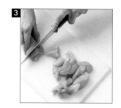 

Crispy Duck with Noodles

This is a robustly flavored dish that makes a substantial entrée. Serve it with a refreshing cucumber salad or lightly stir-fried vegetables.

NUTRITIONAL INFORMATION

Calories	433	Sugars	.........7g
Protein	........25g	Fat	..........10g
Carbohydrate	...59g	Saturates	.......2g

20 mins, plus 1hr marinating   30 mins

SERVES 4

I N G R E D I E N T S

3 duck breasts, total weight about 14 oz/400 g

2 garlic cloves, crushed

1½ tsp chili paste

1 tbsp honey

3 tbsp dark soy sauce

½ tsp five-spice powder

9 oz/250 g rice stick noodles

1 tsp vegetable oil

1 tsp sesame oil

2 scallions, sliced

3½ oz/100 g snow peas

2 tbsp tamarind juice

sesame seeds, to garnish

1 Prick the skin of the duck breasts all over with a fork. Place in a deep dish.

2 Mix together the garlic, chili paste, honey, soy sauce, and five-spice, then pour over the duck breasts. Turn to coat evenly, then cover and marinate in the refrigerator for at least 1 hour.

3 Meanwhile, soak the rice noodles in hot water for 15 minutes. Drain well.

4 Lift the duck breasts from the marinade (reserve the marinade).

Cook on a rack under a hot broiler for about 10 minutes, turning occasionally, until they become a rich golden brown. Transfer the duck breasts to a plate, slice thinly, and keep warm until needed.

5 Heat the vegetable and sesame oils in a skillet, add the sliced scallions and the snow peas, and toss for 2 minutes. Stir in the reserved marinade and the tamarind juice, and bring to a boil.

6 Add the sliced duck and the noodles to the skillet, and toss to heat them thoroughly. Serve immediately, sprinkled with sesame seeds to garnish.

Hot Beef & Coconut Curry

The heat of the chile in this curry is balanced and softened by the coconut milk, producing a creamy-textured, rich, and lavishly spiced dish.

NUTRITIONAL INFORMATION

Calories	230	Sugars	........6g
Protein	........29g	Fat	..........10g
Carbohydrate	....8g	Saturates	.......3g

 15 mins | 40 mins

SERVES 4

INGREDIENTS

1¾ cups coconut milk

2 tbsp Thai red curry paste

2 garlic cloves, crushed

1lb 2 oz/500 g braising steak

2 kaffir lime leaves, shredded

3 tbsp kaffir lime juice

2 tbsp Thai fish sauce

1 large red chile, seeded and sliced

½ tsp turmeric

½ tsp salt

2 tbsp chopped fresh basil

2 tbsp chopped fresh cilantro

shredded coconut, to garnish

boiled rice, to serve

1 Bring the coconut milk to a boil in a large pan. Lower the heat, then simmer gently for 10 minutes to thicken. Stir in the red curry paste and garlic, and simmer for an additional 5 minutes.

2 Cut the beef into ³/₄-inch/2-cm chunks, and add them to the pan. Bring the curry to a boil, stirring constantly, then lower the heat.

3 Add the lime leaves, lime juice, fish sauce, chile, turmeric, and salt. Cover the pan and simmer for 20–25 minutes, until the meat is tender, adding a little water if the sauce looks too dry.

4 Stir in the fresh basil and cilantro, and adjust the seasoning to taste. Sprinkle the curry with coconut and serve immediately with boiled rice.

COOK'S TIP

This recipe uses one of the larger, milder red chile peppers—either fresno or Dutch—simply because they give more color to the dish. If you prefer to use small Thai, or bird-eye, chiles, you will still need only one because they are much hotter.

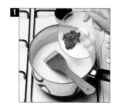

Thai-Style Burgers

If your family likes to eat burgers, try these—they have a much more interesting flavor than conventional hamburgers.

NUTRITIONAL INFORMATION

Calories 358	Sugars 1g	
Protein 23g	Fat 29g	
Carbohydrate 2g	Saturates 5g	

15 mins   8 mins

SERVES 4

INGREDIENTS

1 small lemongrass stem

1 small red chili, seeded

2 garlic cloves, peeled

2 scallions

2⅔ cups closed-cup mushrooms

14 oz/400 g ground pork

1 tbsp Thai fish sauce

3 tbsp chopped fresh cilantro

sunflower oil, for cooking

2 tbsp mayonnaise

1 tbsp lime juice

salt and pepper

TO SERVE

4 sesame hamburger buns

shredded napa cabbage

1 Place the lemongrass, chile, garlic, and scallions in a food processor and process to a smooth paste. Add the mushrooms to the food processor and process until they are chopped very finely.

2 Add the ground pork, fish sauce, and cilantro. Season well with salt and pepper, then divide the mixture into 4 equal portions and use lightly floured hands to shape them into flat burger shapes.

3 Heat the oil in a skillet over medium heat. Add the burgers to the pan and cook for 6–8 minutes, until they are done to your taste.

4 Meanwhile, mix the mayonnaise with the lime juice. Split the hamburger buns and spread the lime-flavored mayonnaise on the cut surfaces. Add a few shredded napa cabbage leaves, top with a burger, and sandwich together. Serve immediately, while still hot.

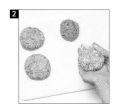

COOK'S TIP

Add a spoonful of your favorite relish to each burger or add a few pieces of crisp pickled vegetables for a change of texture.

Fragrant Black Bean Chili

Enjoy this chili bean stew Mexican style with soft tortillas, or Californian-style in a bowl with crisp tortilla chips crumbled in.

NUTRITIONAL INFORMATION

Calories	428	Sugars	........11g
Protein	........31g	Fat	..........10g
Carbohydrate	...53g	Saturates	.......2g

🥄 20 mins   🕐 2½ hrs

SERVES 4

INGREDIENTS

14 oz/400 g dried black beans, soaked overnight and drained

2 tbsp olive oil

1 onion, chopped

5 garlic cloves, coarsely chopped

2 strips bacon, diced (optional)

½–1 tsp ground cumin

½–1 tsp mild red chili powder

1 red bell pepper, seeded and diced

1 carrot, diced

14 oz/400 g tomatoes, canned and chopped, or fresh and diced

1 bunch fresh cilantro, coarsely chopped

salt and pepper

1 Put the beans in a pan, cover with water, and bring to a boil. Boil for 10 minutes, then lower the heat and simmer for about 1½ hours, until tender. Drain well, reserving scant 1 cup of the cooking liquid.

2 Heat the oil in a skillet. Add the onion and garlic and cook for 2 minutes, stirring. Stir in the bacon, if using, and cook, stirring occasionally, until the bacon is cooked and the onion is soft.

3 Stir in the cumin and chili powder and cook for a few seconds. Add the red bell pepper, carrot, and tomatoes. Cook over medium heat for 5 minutes.

4 Add half the cilantro and the beans with their reserved liquid. Season with salt and pepper. Simmer for 30–45 minutes, or until thickened.

5 Stir through the remaining cilantro, adjust the seasoning to taste, and serve at once.

COOK'S TIP

For speed you could use canned beans: drain off the liquid from the can and use 1 cup water for the liquid added in step 4.

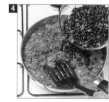

Spicy Pork with Prunes

Prunes add an earthy, wine flavor to this spicy stew. Serve with corn tortillas or crusty bread to dip into the rich sauce.

NUTRITIONAL INFORMATION

Calories	352	Sugars 1g
Protein	. . . . .39g	Fat 12g
Carbohydrate	. . .24g	Saturates 9g

🌶 🌶 🌶

15 mins, plus 8 hrs marinating   🕐   3 hrs 50 mins

SERVES 4–6

I N G R E D I E N T S

3 lb 5 oz/1.5 kg pork joint, such as leg or shoulder

juice of 2–3 limes

10 garlic cloves, chopped

3–4 tbsp mild chili powder, such as ancho or New Mexico

4 tbsp vegetable oil

2 onions, chopped

generous 2 cups chicken bouillon

25 small, tart tomatoes, coarsely chopped

25 prunes, pitted

1–2 tsp sugar

pinch of ground cinnamon

pinch of ground allspice

pinch of ground cumin

salt

warmed corn tortillas, to serve

1 Combine the pork with the lime juice, garlic, chili powder, and half the oil in a nonmetallic bowl. Season with salt. Cover and marinate in the refrigerator overnight.

2 Remove the pork from the marinade, wipe dry with paper towels, and reserve the marinade. Heat the remaining oil in a flameproof casserole and brown the pork evenly, until just golden. Add the onions, reserved marinade, and the bouillon. Cover and cook in a preheated oven, 350°F/180°C, for 2–3 hours, until tender.

3 Spoon off the fat from the surface of the cooking liquid and add the tomatoes. Continue to cook for 20 minutes, or until the tomatoes are tender. Mash the tomatoes into a coarse paste. Add the prunes, sugar, and spices to taste.

4 Increase the oven temperature to 400°F/200°C. Cook the meat and sauce in the oven, uncovered, for 20–30 minutes, until the meat has browned and the juices have thickened.

5 Remove the meat from the pan and let it stand for a few minutes. Carve into thin slices, and spoon the sauce over the top. Serve with warm tortillas.

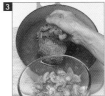

Wild Mushroom Vermicelli

Simple to make, this spicy dish has Spanish chorizo sausage and anchovies as its main ingredients, and will set the taste buds tingling.

NUTRITIONAL INFORMATION

Calories 495	Sugars 1g
Protein 15g	Fat 35g
Carbohydrate ...33g	Saturates 5g

   5 mins   10 mins

SERVES 6

I N G R E D I E N T S

1½ lb/680 g dried vermicelli

½ cup olive oil

2 garlic cloves, finely chopped

4½ oz/125 g chorizo, sliced

8 oz/225 g wild mushrooms

3 fresh red chiles, seeded and chopped

2 tbsp freshly grated Parmesan cheese

salt and pepper

10 anchovy fillets, to garnish

1 Bring a large pan of lightly salted water to a boil. Add the vermicelli and 1 tablespoon of the oil, and cook until just tender but still firm to the bite. Drain, place on a large, warm serving plate, and keep warm.

2 Meanwhile heat the remaining oil in a large skillet. Add the garlic and cook for 1 minute. Add the chorizo and wild mushrooms and cook for 4 minutes, then add the chopped red chiles and cook for another minute, until the mushrooms are just cooked through.

3 Pour the chorizo and wild mushroom mixture over the vermicelli and season with a little salt and pepper. Sprinkle over freshly grated Parmesan cheese, garnish with the anchovy fillets, and serve immediately.

COOK'S TIP

Always obtain wild mushrooms from a reliable source and never pick them yourself unless you are absolutely certain of their identity.

Lamb Couscous

Couscous is a North African specialty. It is usually accompanied by a spicy mixture of meat and fruit, which adds a note of luxury.

NUTRITIONAL INFORMATION

Calories	647	Sugars	........22g
Protein	........41g	Fat	..........21g
Carbohydrate	...79g	Saturates	......6g

20 mins • 20 mins

SERVES 4

I N G R E D I E N T S

2 tbsp olive oil

1 lb 2 oz/500 g lean lamb sirloin, thinly sliced

2 onions, sliced

2 garlic cloves, chopped

1 cinnamon stick

1 tsp ground ginger

1 tsp paprika

½ tsp chili powder

2½ cups hot chicken bouillon

3 carrots, thinly sliced

2 turnips, halved and sliced

14 oz/400 g canned chopped tomatoes

2 tbsp raisins

15 oz/425 g canned garbanzo beans, drained and rinsed

3 zucchini, sliced

4½ oz/125 g fresh dates, halved and pitted, or 4½ oz/125 g dried apricots

1¾ cups couscous

2½ cups boiling water

salt

  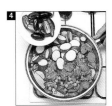

1 Heat the oil in a skillet and cook the lamb briskly for 3 minutes, until browned. Remove from the skillet with a slotted spoon, and set aside.

2 Add the onions to the pan and cook, stirring constantly, until soft. Add the garlic and spices and cook for 1 minute.

3 Add the bouillon, carrots, turnips, tomatoes, raisins, garbanzo beans, lamb, and salt to taste. Cover, bring to a boil, and simmer for 12 minutes.

4 Add the zucchini and the dates. Cover again and cook for 8 minutes.

5 Meanwhile, put the couscous in a bowl with 1 teaspoon of salt and pour the boiling water over it. Let soak for 5 minutes, then fluff it with a fork.

6 To serve, pile the couscous onto a warmed serving platter and make a hollow in the center. Put the meat and vegetables in the hollow (discard the cinnamon stick), and pour some sauce over it. Serve the rest of the sauce separately.

Spiced Lamb & Lentils

This recipe makes a hearty, warming winter curry. Gram lentils are used in this recipe but field yellow peas make a tasty alternative.

NUTRITIONAL INFORMATION

Calories	397	Sugars	.........1g
Protein	........42g	Fat	..........22g
Carbohydrate	....8g	Saturates	......9g

20 mins, plus 6 hrs soaking   1¼ hrs

SERVES 4

INGREDIENTS

2 tbsp oil

1 tsp cumin seeds

2 bay leaves

1-inch/2.5-cm piece cinnamon stick

1 onion, chopped

1 lb 10 oz/750 g lean, boneless lamb, cut into 1-inch/2.5-cm cubes

⅔ cup split gram lentils, soaked for 6 hours and drained

1 tsp salt

1 fresh green chile, seeded and sliced

5½ cups water

1 garlic clove, crushed

¼ tsp ground turmeric

1 tsp chili powder

½ tsp garam masala or curry powder (optional)

1 tbsp chopped fresh cilantro (optional)

nan bread and pickles, to serve

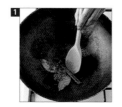

1   Heat the oil in a balti pan or a wok, add the cumin seeds, bay leaves, and cinnamon stick, and cook over high heat, until the cumin seeds start popping.

2   Add the onion and stir-fry until golden brown. Add the cubed lamb to the pan, and stir-fry until evenly browned.

3   Add the lentils, salt, chile, water, garlic, turmeric, and chili powder, and stir well. Bring the mixture to a boil, then simmer for 1 hour, stirring occasionally.

4   Season with garam masala, if using, and cook for another 5 minutes. Remove and discard the cinnamon stick.

5   Stir in the chopped cilantro, if using, and serve with nans and pickles.

COOK'S TIP

To save time on soaking, use 14 oz/400 g canned lentils. These should be added to the curry when it has finished cooking. Heat through gently until the lentils are hot, then garnish and serve.

Melon & Ginger Crush

A really refreshing summer drink, this melon crush is quick and simple to make. Use ordinary limes if you cannot find kaffir limes.

NUTRITIONAL INFORMATION

Calories 46   Sugars 7g
Protein . . . . .1g   Fat 0g
Carbohydrate . . . .7g   Saturates 0g

 5 mins   0 mins

SERVES 4

I N G R E D I E N T S

1 melon, about 1 lb 12 oz/800 g

6 tbsp ginger wine

3 tbsp kaffir lime juice

crushed ice

1 lime

1 Peel and seed the melon and roughly chop the flesh. Place it in a blender or food processor with the ginger wine and the lime juice.

2 Blend on high speed, until the mixture is completely smooth.

3 Put plenty of crushed ice into 4 tall glasses. Pour the melon and ginger crush over the ice.

4 Cut the lime into slim slices, cut a slit in each one, and slip one onto the rim of each glass. Serve immediately.

VARIATION

For a nonalcoholic version of this drink, omit the ginger wine, then top off the glass with ginger ale. For a seasonal change of flavor, use a watermelon.

Lychee & Ginger Sherbet

A refreshing dessert after a rich meal, this quick and simple sherbet can be served alone or with fruit salad.

NUTRITIONAL INFORMATION

Calories . . . . 159 Sugars 40g
Protein . . . . .2g Fat 0g
Carbohydrate . . .40g Saturates 0g

5 mins, plus 5-6 hrs freezing

0 mins

SERVES 4

I N G R E D I E N T S

1 lb 12 oz/800 g canned lychees in syrup

zest of 1 lime, finely grated

2 tbsp lime juice

3 tbsp candied ginger syrup

2 egg whites

T O   D E C O R A T E

starfruit slices

slivers of candied ginger

1 Drain the lychees, reserving the syrup. Place the fruits in a blender or a food processor with the lime zest, lime juice, and candied ginger syrup, and process until completely smooth. Transfer to a mixing bowl and pour in the reserved lychee syrup.

2 To make the sherbet, pour the mixture into a freezerproof container and freeze for 1–1½ hours, until slushy in texture. Remove from the freezer and whisk to break up the ice crystals. Whisk the egg whites in a clean, dry bowl, until they rise in stiff peaks, then fold quickly and lightly into the iced mixture. Return the mixture to the freezer and freeze until firm. Alternatively, to save time, replace the whole procedure in this step by processing the mixture quickly in an ice-cream maker.

3 When ready to serve, remove the sherbet from the freezer and place in the refrigerator 20 minutes before needed. Serve in scoops, decorated with slices of starfruit and slivers of candied ginger.

COOK'S TIP

It is not recommended that raw egg whites are served to very young children, pregnant women, the elderly, or anyone weakened by chronic illness.